POSTCARDS FROM HOME

Sylvia Morice

Copyright © 2012 Sylvia Morice
All rights reserved.
ISBN: **1480134074**
ISBN-13: **978-1480134072**

DEDICATION

To my wonderful children, Shane and Erin, for putting up with a mother who liked to make up or embellish stories about them when they were growing up, I say thank you.

And as always, to Gary, the love of my life.

CONTENTS

	Acknowledgements	i
1	Eating My Words	Pg 1
2	A New Era	Pg 5
3	Father's Day	Pg 9
4	The More Things Change	Pg 12
5	Heading To The Cottage	Pg 16
6	Rising To a Challenge	Pg 20
7	Out of The Mouths of Babes	Pg 24
8	Trade Places, Anyone?	Pg 28
9	I'll Be Ready For Halloween	Pg 31
10	Home For The Holidays	Pg 36
11	Overcoming Envy	Pg 44
12	Tokens of Undying Love	Pg 48
13	Do You Work?	Pg 52
14	Going Home	Pg 57
15	Life With a Colicky Kid	Pg 64
16	One Mother's Day	Pg 68
17	Letter To Santa	Pg 71
18	First Week of School	Pg 77
19	Do Not Walk On This Surface	Pg 80
20	Honey, We've Been Transferred	Pg 84
21	Mom, Can We Have a Puppy?	Pg 89
	About The Author	Pg 95

ACKNOWLEDGMENTS

The inspiration for the material in Postcards From Home came, first of all, from my experiences of being the mother of two precocious children. From this vantage point I used creative licence to embellish and fictionalize events from our daily lives and turn them into this collection of short stories and essays. I hope you enjoy reading them.

EATING MY WORDS

When my children were small I made the mistake of saying, "I'm so fortunate; Shane and Erin eat everything I put in front of them."

These words have come back to haunt me. My children are no longer tiny babies eating pureed peas, or even cute little toddlers munching on carrot sticks or arrowroot cookies no one else wanted anyway.

They have evolved into walking, talking, "I'll grab the kitchen stool and help myself," eating machines, devouring food like piranhas in a feeding frenzy.

"What's for supper, Mom?" Shane asks at the breakfast table.

"What's in my lunch-box?" asks Erin.

"May we have an after-school snack?"

"What can we nibble on before bedtime?"

This vicious cycle never ends.

Other mothers stare in wonderment as my children polish off a second serving of dinner.

"You're so lucky," one mother says to me. "My little Johnny will only eat peanut butter."

Another mother agrees. "I wish my Susie would take a lesson from Shane and Erin, but she refuses to eat anything except toast and strawberry jam."

How I envy those mothers. What a joy it must be to have children who say, "No thanks, I don't want any," or "Mom, I don't like that yucky stuff!"

My children never turn down the offer of food, no matter what it is.

"Grapefruit? Great!"

"Olives? We love olives!"

"Slippery mushrooms and stir-fried broccoli--when do we eat?"

Supper is at five-thirty every night.

"Are you full?" I say at the end of the meal.

"I'm stuffed," says Shane.

"Couldn't eat another bite," adds Erin.

An hour later my son complains of feeling faint and needs two slices of toast, a bowl of butterscotch ice cream and a large glass of milk to save him from starvation.

Just as he's wiping off his milk mustache my daughter comes down from her bath.

"What's for my snack, Mom?" she says. "I'm starved."

Sometimes I yearn for the good old days (the days before we had children), when my husband and I could eat anything we wanted, without feeling guilty or being interrogated.

Now if we share a late-night pizza or a midnight bag of salt-and-vinegar potato chips we're faced with an inquisition in the morning.

Shane and Erin bound downstairs, sniffing like hound dogs.

"What do I smell?" Erin says.

"Nothing," I reply. I can't look her in the eye.

"Yes, I do," she says, her little nose twitching. "You and Daddy had PIZZA last night!!!"

How do they know? We take great care to be discreet. We stuff our dirty dishes into the dishwasher and hide the pizza box in the garage cupboard. We deodorize the house, vacuum up the crumbs, and scrub the sauce stains off our clothes.

If only I hadn't carelessly tossed that small piece of leftover crust into the kitchen garbage can!

Last summer we were at a restaurant with my mother. She was being a good Grammy; she cut my children's meat and buttered their rolls.

Shane eyed her food. "What do you have, Grammy?"

"Baked scallops with tartar sauce," she said. "Would you like to try a bite?"

My husband fixed her with an icy stare and I shook my head.

"No Mom," I said, "that's not a good idea."

"Why not, dear--is Shane allergic to scallops?"

"Oh, it's nothing like that," I said. "We're just afraid he might LIKE them!"

I'm not looking forward to the upcoming years; in fact, I have nightmares about having to feed ravenous teenagers. In my nightmares I meet a friend on the street and she stares at me.

"My, you're thin," she says, "just skin-and-bones. Have you been ill?"

"No," I say, "I just have teenagers in my house."

If the friend is also a mother of teenagers she nods her head sagely, pats my arm and says, "Say no more, dear, say no more."

I wake from this dream in a cold sweat and head downstairs to the kitchen for a drink of water. Then I remember the piece of chocolate cake I stashed in the pots and pans cupboard after supper--chocolate cake certainly tastes delicious in the dark.

Last evening my husband and I had a lively discussion about our family's food bills, and words such as "outrageous", "exorbitant" and "poorhouse" cropped up.

"Remember when Shane and Erin were babies?" I said, trying to melt the frost in the room, "and I bragged about how lucky we were because they ate everything and anything we gave them?"

"Uh-huh."

"Who would have guessed I'd end up wishing I could eat my words?"

"We both might have to eat your words." My husband threw this remark over his shoulder on his way to the kitchen. "The children have devoured everything else in the house."

"No, they haven't," I said. "They didn't find the bag of salt-and-vinegar potato chips I hid in the freezer."

My husband grinned. "Chips? Great!" he said, as he descended the basement stairs. "I'm starved."

The vicious cycle continues.

A NEW ERA

I have now entered a whole new era in my life.

No longer am I the busy, overworked mother of active preschool children; no, I am the, "What do you do at home all day?" mother whose children are at school from eight in the morning 'til three-thirty in the afternoon.

People who were once sympathetic to my various complaints and concerns (mothers of other preschool children), now eye me suspiciously, especially at the supermarket.

As I stroll up and down the aisles on Thursday mornings they stare at me, begrudging the fact that I no longer have to say, "No Erin, put that sugar-coated cereal back", or "Shane, you know we don't eat fortified imitation chicken at our house."

Even my husband claims I'm spoiled now that I don't have children tagging along with me everywhere I go.

Once in a while he accompanies me to the grocery store and he becomes upset when I say, "No dear, put that bag of chocolate cookies back where you found it," or "Now dear, you know we don't eat fortified imitation bacon at our house."

He says it's embarrassing to be treated like a child, but if he would hold onto the cart handle and be a good boy like I told him to he wouldn't find himself in these situations!

At the checkout last Thursday, Marion, mother of two-year-old Jeffrey and four-year-old Sally, voiced her disgust outright at the carefree, calm way I lifted my groceries out of the shopping cart.

I think she was upset because she had found three candy bars and two small bags of potato chips tucked into her grocery order while I wasn't finding ANY surprises in mine.

"What do you do at home all day alone?" Marion snarled as she bent to grab a package of bubblegum out of little Jeffrey's hand. "You must find the time awfully long and boring."

"Not at all," I said. "Between my massage at the local spa every morning and my afternoon bridge parties I manage to keep busy."

Poor Marion stood at the counter with her mouth hanging open and a look of "Are you serious or not?" on her face.

Little did she know what I've been through in the trenches; if only she had a few hours to spare I could have regaled her with tales of my kids' exploits in the supermarket.

The bright fluorescent lights and crowds of people in the stores make my children think they're in a theatre—and they adore being on center stage!

They absolutely love an audience; in fact they often hold talent shows in my living room and recruit neighborhood children to applaud their routines.

They see humor in almost every situation and if there is no humor to be found they do their best to create some, using whatever means is necessary.

I could have told Marion about one memorable trip to our local market when my son Shane and I were standing at a checkout behind a woman whom I would describe as "full figured". Eagle-eyed Shane noticed her immediately.

"Look, Mommy," he said in his four-year-old voice. "Is that lady ever FAT!"

At this point I tapped him ever-so-gently on the arm and whispered, "Sh-hh-hh."

Shane was indignant. "What did you hit me for, Mommy?" he yelled. "She really IS fat!"

After we arrived home, I took the time, as any good mother would, to explain to my little son how we must not call people names or talk about them in public. His little blond head bobbed up and down to show that he understood.

I also explained that it isn't nice to hurt someone's feelings on purpose.

That was the clincher, I thought. *He won't do that again.*

A few weeks later Shane was back at the supermarket with his father, when of course they came across another woman of generous proportions.

My son eyed her closely, but remained silent.

My husband breathed a sigh of relief and they were just about to leave the store when the dear boy tugged at his father's arm for attention and loudly exclaimed, "Wasn't I good, Daddy? I didn't even call her FAT!"

My husband left the supermarket as quickly as possible and since then has refused to go grocery shopping with any person under the age of twenty-one!

Oh yes, Marion, I've paid my dues; I deserve my supermarket solitude.

I could have told her about the time my son pulled out the bottom can of spaghetti from an aisle display, or I could have mentioned how my children played Frisbee with a ready-to-bake-pizza they found next to the sliced salami, or how they often managed to disappear from sight (sometimes right out of the store), while I was busy paying for the groceries, or even how my son once managed to sample six flavors of yogurt before the store manager plucked him out of the cooler and returned him to my cart.

I'm sure it would have lightened Marion's heart and soul to hear my pitiful tales, but she had no time, and I had no time.

Marion paid cash for her groceries and left the store quickly, dragging Jeffrey by one hand and little Sally by the other. Both children were trying to wiggle out of her grasp and crying, "But Mommy, we WANT bubblegum that tastes like dill pickles!"

I was in a hurry, too.

I drove home, carried in and put away my fourteen bags of groceries, folded the last load of laundry from the dryer and sprayed my oven for its yearly (whether it needs it or not), cleaning. What a life of debauchery I lead.

Too bad I don't' know how to play bridge.

FATHER'S DAY

My children love Father's Day—that special day gives them a chance to express their deep feelings for the man who fathered them, helps nurture them, works hard to feed and clothe them, and takes the time to play Snakes and Ladders or basketball with them.

Once a year Dad deserves a day of rest, recognition, and recreation; my kids are especially keen on the recreation aspect.

"Let's go fishing on Father's Day," they say.

Now there's a treat for Dad—spend an afternoon fishing with two young children and a greying wife, none of whom will bait their own hooks.

He can look forward to untangling nylon lines, replacing bobbers and lead weights that disappear faster than socks in my washing machine, and if any member of our little group is fortunate enough to actually land a fish, Dad gets to kill it (while the rest of us turn our heads), and clean it when we arrive back home.

All that and a card, too! It's almost more affection than one man can handle.

Dad starts getting edgy a few days before Father's Day.

I catch him hiding his fishing gear in the back of the den closet and tossing around such remarks as, "You know dear, I have so many ties; did you know I have fifty ties?" or "I certainly do have a LOT of shirts, don't I, dear? I'm so glad I don't need ANY new shirts."

I smile at him. "Yes," I say, "but you can always use more socks and undershorts," and then I watch as his expression turns to, *Oh, no--not undershorts and socks again this year for Father's Day.*

The fateful morning arrives.

"Happy Father's Day, Daddy," the children shout as they rush into our bedroom at 7:09 am.

"Daddy, wake up, Daddy—we have a busy day ahead; we're taking you FISHING!"

Dad is served breakfast in bed: white coffee (too much milk), orange pop (it fizzes better than orange juice and the children like to watch that), and a bagel that has been microwaved into solid granite.

Shane and Erin sit at the bottom of the bed to make sure that Dad eats and drinks everything on the Queen Elizabeth II souvenir tray.

Dad opens his cards, reads the verses out loud (in unison with the children, who have them memorized), and remembers to express his surprise and delight when he unwraps navy blue socks and a matching tie.

He is now the proud owner of fifty-one ties!

"We hope you like them, Dad," the children chime. "Mom helped us pick them out."

I try not to grin.

'Dad' treats me to a look that clearly promises, "I'll get even, you know. You have a birthday coming up next month."

"Happy Father's Day, darling," I whisper. "Now get up; the children are waiting for you to help them dig worms."

THE MORE THINGS CHANGE

I feel nostalgic in January.

For some reason heading into a new year full of hopes and possibilities makes me pause and recall past years; things have certainly changed since I was a child growing up in rural Canada in the 1950s and 60s.

Home was a fourteen-room farmhouse complete with stained glass windows, turned oak newel posts on a winding staircase, wainscoting in the dining room and two oil-guzzling furnaces that helped keep my family warm, but poor.

The property boasted a huge barn, a chicken coop where my father also kept an old-fashioned grinding wheel he used to sharpen his scary-looking axe, and a long driveway lined with maple, birch and chestnut trees.

This long driveway became a mire of mud every spring and filled with deep snowdrifts every winter.

I liked winter when I was a little girl; I especially liked to make snow angels in the pristine country snow that stuck like glue to my woolen pants and jacket.

After I finished playing outside I'd arrive at the kitchen door, frozen to the bone and covered from head to toe with snow.

My mother guarded her house and in the winter met her children at the door with her sentry broom.

"Turn around," she'd say, and I'd rotate, arms held high above my head in surrender, then straight out like a scarecrow, then solder-like at my sides while my mother swept at me with her corn broom.

We stripped off my wool hat and mittens to drip in the porcelain sink, then transferred them to the warming oven above the oil stove to dry overnight.

Today I stand in the living room of my energy-efficient home and look out the window.

In the front yard my children toss snowballs at each other. The snow hits, then slides easily off their nylon snowsuits back to the ground where it belongs.

Shane and Erin come to the door several times.

"No, Mom, we don't want to come in yet; we just need dry mittens."

Back they scoot to their snow fort, their hands warm and dry once again.

I gather up the assortment of mittens, two pairs from each child, and toss them into the clothes dryer. I have no oil stove in my kitchen and my children have never seen a warming oven.

After a while I call the children in for an early supper because their skating lessons start at six o'clock.

My children are learning to skate with at least eighty other children on man-made ice in an enclosed rink, gliding around the ice surface to the voice of Kermit the Frog singing "The Rainbow Connection."

I tie their skates for them then sit with other shivering parents and wait to untie them at the end of the hour's lesson.

I learned to skate on a frozen swamp at the back of our farm property.

The ice was bumpy, full of air pockets and often covered with snow, but that didn't matter to me.

My brothers, sister and I would skate and fall down because of the bumps, skate and trip in a crack in the ice, skate and crash into a snow bank or a clump of bushes at the edge of the ice and skate and fall backwards.

We didn't wear helmets when I was growing up, and sometimes we cracked our heads on the ice so hard that we could taste blood, and the world roared in our ears.

We'd lie on the ice for a few moments until the pain subsided and we'd regained enough balance and nerve to skate again, then off we would go.

We'd stay out on the ice until our fingers ached and our cheeks and feet were numb, and then finally one of us would cry out, "My feet are frozen; I can't feel my toes...and I want to go hommmme."

Home was a quarter of a mile away, up a hill. So up we'd trudge, exhausted and cold, anxious to warm our hands and feet at the kitchen oil stove and our insides with hot chocolate our mother made.

Mom added milk and cocoa to a blue enameled pot, set it to heat on the oil stove for a few minutes and then poured the steaming liquid into cups.

My children love hot chocolate, too.

I pour cold milk into their personalized stoneware mugs, add a squirt of the chocolate syrup I keep in the cupboard and stick the mugs into the microwave for two minutes on high power—delicious, but not at all the same as the hot chocolate I enjoyed as a child.

Reminiscing about my childhood has made me realize that some things haven't changed all that much since I was a child.

Today's children love skating, snowball-fighting and sledding every bit as much as past generations of children did; they also enjoy cross-country skiing and, gulp, snow-boarding.

Equipment has certainly changed over the years, but children haven't.

My children don't seem to know they should come inside before they're frozen to the bone, they enjoy sucking on icicles broken off the patio roof with a stick and they catch snowflakes on their tongues.

They shout with glee when school is cancelled because of a storm and they track snow into the house if I don't stop them at the door.

Perhaps the old adage is true: *The more things change, the more they stay the same.*

I think of that adage now as I repeat to myself for the ninth time today the words spoken in the winter by my mother when I was a child--"I'll be SO glad when spring arrives!"

HEADING TO THE COTTAGE

It was a hot afternoon in the car.

Traffic was heavy.

There were long lines of tractor trailers, vans and motor homes pulling sub-compact cars and SUVs.

There was also a vast assortment of vehicles hauling travel trailers, hardtop campers and utility trailers overflowing with gas barbeques, lawn chairs and children's bicycles.

Everyone was in a hurry to get to their cottages and lakeside campsites before the holiday traffic began.

I looked out my car window. We were IN the holiday traffic--right smack in the middle of it, like warm ham between slices of rye bread.

What had we been thinking?

For some unknown reason two fairly intelligent adults decided it would be a good idea to drive to our cottage, hundreds of kilometers away from our comfortable home, on the eve of a major national holiday.

We were towing one of the aforementioned utility trailers stuffed with the aforementioned gas barbecues, lawn chairs and children's bicycles. (Did I forget to mention the diving gear, nine-by-nine tourist tent, sleeping bags, sheets of glass and cans of paint and stain?)

Our full-size car trunk was also crammed with board games, suitcases, an electric frying pan, a vacuum cleaner, rain boots and extra sneakers for the entire family and sundry power tools for my husband to play with at the cottage.

The trunk lid barely closed, and there was absolutely NO room for mundane items such as food.

"Never mind, dear," said my husband when I complained about our lack of culinary supplies. "We'll be at the cottage in plenty of time to get the car unpacked so you can catch the grocery store before it closes."

"Certainly," I said. "I'll only have to backtrack fifty kilometers to the nearest town. No problem. I'm sure that as long as I get my foot in the door no decent store manager will throw me out; I'm good at looking pathetic."

"You sure are, dear," my husband agreed, and smiled as if he'd just handed me a dozen roses. "Good thing we're getting away early."

Yes, the drive was progressing nicely.

We had already traveled for one hour, had refereed only three major fights in the back seat and had munched our way through an entire loaf of sandwiches, four containers of juice, six apples and two 200 gram bags of potato chips—one regular and one salt-and-vinegar.

This was turning out to be a good trip.

Suddenly my husband turned to me. "Shut the music off for a minute," he said above the loud, clear voice of Rita MacNeil.

As soon as I silenced Rita I could hear a terrible roaring noise, like a stock car racing at full speed. I knew immediately what the problem was.

After all, we WERE starting our annual vacation, we HAD drained our bank account to finance this little trip and we WERE in a hurry to reach the tranquility of our ocean-view cottage. Of course that meant we would have car trouble.

"It's the muffler, right?" I said to my husband, who was gripping the steering wheel like a ship-wreck survivor clutching a life preserver in a choppy sea.

I received a grunt as a reply and took that to mean, "Yes."

Meanwhile, the roar increased. Every time my husband pressed the accelerator, the car vibrated.

"We'll have to stop up ahead and get this fixed," hubby said. "There goes at least $150, you know!" (This was said in a tone of voice that vaguely suggested the problem was somehow MY fault.)

We roared along the highway for another thirty kilometers until we reached the nearest town.

I'll spare you the trying details of finding a repair shop that was willing to fix our muffler on the eve of a national holiday. Suffice it to say that three hours later and $157.95 poorer we were back on the road, with Rita's "Fast Train to Tokyo" the only sound vibrating our car now.

My husband and I began to relax as the kilometers sped by. Even the children were content; they were busily munching on cheese puffs and moving their bodies to the rhythm of Rita's music.

We were really making progress. Traffic was moving along steadily. Happy cottage thoughts were beginning to surface in my mind.

My head became filled with images of warm days and cool nights, the sound of raindrops bouncing off the cottage roof, eating lobster outdoors at the picnic table, hearing the children laugh as waves washed over them, and taking long peaceful walks with my husband along the shoreline at sunset.

"Life is good indeed," I said, sighing contentedly.

Unfortunately, Life heard me.

"Mommy," our little girl yelled from the back seat. "Tell Daddy to stop the car--I think I'm going to throw up!"

RISING TO A CHALLENGE

Friends dropped in to visit recently. We sat around my kitchen table, shared coffee and cinnamon buns and discussed politics, the weather, business and squirrels.

It seems that my friends had a squirrel living in their backyard, and this squirrel was neither a welcome pet nor an invited guest.

He spent his days running up and down tree trunks, scampering onto branches just out of reach of the family dogs, and there he'd sit, chattering insults to the two frenzied canines below, driving the dogs to the edge of insanity and then trying to push them over.

As if tormenting family pets wasn't bad enough, the squirrel also stole.

He snatched food from the dogs' dishes and performed raids on the bird feeder that was conveniently nestled in a nearby tree, stuffing his cheeks with delicious sunflower seeds.

One day my friends said, "Enough is enough, Mr. Squirrel; those seeds are meant for the birds, not for you," and they decided to take action.

"This problem is easy to fix," they said, rising to the challenge. "All we need to do is remove the bird feeder from the tree."

So they did.

They stuck an old metal pole into the ground and fastened the bird feeder to the top of it.

The squirrel was not bothered in the least. Apparently he too could rise to a challenge, and he quickly took charge of the situation.

He looked at the pole as if to say: "If what I want is at the top of that pole, then the top of that pole is where I go."

It was not an easy climb. The metal pole was rusted in spots, which provided a little bit of traction, but overall, there wasn't much of anything for him to grip onto.

The little squirrel dug his nails in for dear life and tried over and over again to scale new heights.

It took several attempts, but finally his perseverance paid off and he reached the top, rewarding himself with more crunchy sunflower seeds.

Cheeks stuffed with booty, he scampered back down the pole and up a tree, presumably to stash his loot into a little squirrel cupboard for the winter.

My friends couldn't stand to be outdone by a squirrel, so they took the challenge one step further, exchanging the metal pole for a slippery plastic pipe.

"It should be impossible for any squirrel to climb this," my friends said, but unfortunately they forgot to mention this to the squirrel.

The little squirrel took charge again; he stared at the pole, planning his strategy.

He backed away a few meters then charged at the pole, managing to climb up a meter or so before he slipped back down to base camp.

He backed up farther next time, all the way to the fence.

On your mark, get set, GO!

Once again, victory belonged to the squirrel, and he stuffed his cheeks with the spoils of the skirmish.

"Okay, Buster," said my friends, "You may have won the battle, but you haven't won the war."

The ultimate solution seemed simple and my friends wondered why they hadn't thought of it before.

They drilled a hole in the middle of a large metal tray and put it on the pole, near the top but underneath the feeder.

"That is the end, Mr. Squirrel," they said smugly, and congratulated themselves on their ingenuity.

The next time the larcenous squirrel scampered up the pole, my friends watched from their kitchen window.

BONK!

The surprised squirrel craned his neck to look up.

"Where did that thing come from?" he seemed to say.

He tried again. BONK! And again, finally pausing as if to think, "I know Heaven is up there, but how do I reach it?"

My friends prepared to celebrate.

They knew that no matter how hard the little squirrel tried, he wouldn't be able to climb over the obstacle put in his way. Heaven would remain forever out of reach.

But once again my friends neglected to inform the squirrel.

Oh, it was true the squirrel couldn't reach his goal by going up the pole. That only got him BONKED on the head.

So...he...goes...down.

He climbs out to the tip of the branch closest to the bird feeder, spreads his little arms and legs and parachutes onto the feeder's peaked roof.

This daring action requires a lot of courage. It tends to knock the wind out of the squirrel when he lands, and there's always the possibility he'll miscalculate the distance and will plummet to the ground instead, but he jumps anyway.

So far he hasn't missed his target.

My friends finally admitted defeat.

"Anyone or anything so determined to reach a goal deserves to succeed," they said.

"The birds and the dogs will simply have to adjust."

We chuckled with our friends when they told us this story.

No one came right out and said so, but I'm quite certain the consensus around the table was that squirrels should be admired, no matter how much of a nuisance they can sometimes be.

After all, they keep their minds on their goals, they overcome huge obstacles mounted in their way, and they don't give up, even after they've been knocked on the head a few times for their efforts.

Maybe humans could learn a thing or two from squirrels.

OUT OF THE MOUTHS OF BABES

All right, I confess. I'm guilty. Out of the mouths of babes come great words—and I steal them. It's a weakness of mine, a flaw in my character.

Words throw themselves at me to stick like cobwebs and I'm forced to write them down. I don't purposely pilfer from my children, but my flesh is weak.

Take last Friday evening, for example.

I sat at the dining room table with my notebook in front of me. It was time to be creative.

I sought inspiration. Nothing.

I stared at the wallpaper. I doodled in my notebook. Precious writing minutes were being wasted.

A sibling argument in the family room caught my attention.

I heard my children's loud voices and my husband's even louder one.

Then silence.

My daughter Erin stomped into the dining room; her hands were clenched into fists and she spoke through gritted teeth.

"I'm so mad at Shane I could hit him! I'd hit him really hard, too. Then see how he'd like it!" she said.

Her words came out in a hiss, like an angry snake.

Fortunately, I remembered advice from my child psychology books.

"Why don't you draw a picture of how you feel?" I said to my daughter. "That would be better than hitting someone."

"Okay, I will," she agreed, but said it in a tone of voice that warned, "Just-you-wait-and-see."

Experience told me this was not a good sign.

Erin ran into my office/laundry room and returned with a piece of plain white paper and a felt marker pen, then quickly scribbled, scribbled, scribbled angry black circles onto the pristine white.

Good, I thought, as I watched discreetly from my spot at the table, *my little girl has finally learned to vent her feelings constructively.*

But black circles were not nearly enough to quench a seven-year-old's thirst for revenge.

Erin suddenly stopped scribbling and looked up at me.

"If Shane had a paper face," she said, "I'd do this to him."

And with those words, she crumpled the paper into a lumpy ball between her fists, walked over to the kitchen garbage can, and threw it in.

Wow.

I'm ashamed to admit that my immediate reaction to this scene was not, *Oh my, how can one small child hold so much anger*, or even, *Well, at least she didn't punch her brother in the stomach like she did the last time.*

It was, *WOW, what a great line for a poem! 'If I had a paper face'....I must write that down.*

Within a few hours I had a new poem written; it was about rejection and anger.

Its first line began, "If I had a paper face...."

The next day I mailed the poem to the editor of a literary magazine in hopes of publication.

I included my name, address, telephone number and stamped self-addressed envelope—but I neglected to identify myself as a woman who steals from little children.

This wasn't an isolated incident, either; I've stolen before.

Last summer I had an article published that began, "It was a hot afternoon in the car," and it pains me now to have to admit that those words were first spoken by my daughter during a long drive from our home to our cottage.

I remember thinking at the time, "What a great opening sentence," and I filed it away to use as my own.

I did use it, too, without giving any credit to Erin; I'm such a bad mother.

I could list even more examples of my purloining, but I'd likely run out of paper if I did, so suffice it to say that the list would be long.

I am so ashamed.

If I ever become financially independent because of my writing, I'll be sure to make restitution to my innocent children; maybe I'll double their allowances.

For now though, I'll try to regain my integrity. I'll strive to be original. I'll do my best not to plagiarize the words of my loved ones.

I promise.

"What's that, Shane? Your sister just erased your favorite computer game? You think she did it on purpose? If Erin was a computer you'd break her into bits and bytes and pull her plug?"

What a great idea for a story! I must go write that down!

TRADE PLACES, ANYONE?

"Wouldn't it be fun," my daughter Erin said at the supper table last night, "if everyone in our family traded places? Shane could go to work and Daddy could go to school. You could go to school, too, Mommy, and I'll stay home and look after Tara."

"Is that what you think I do all day?" I asked. "Look after the dog?"

"No," Erin said. "You do housework, too."

My husband raised his eyebrows and looked around the kitchen.

I knew what he was thinking.

"I'll have you know," I grunted, "I have more important things than just housework to worry about."

"Sure you do, Mom," said Shane. "What's for dessert?"

I gave my son an evil-eye stare and dished up the apple crisp.

"Do you really think I spend every day with my arms full of laundry and my head in a toilet?"

"I know you don't do laundry every day," said Erin, "because my favorite jeans weren't clean this morning. Did you wash them yet, Mom?"

I ignored her question.

"Now children," said my husband. "You know that your mother is a busy woman. It takes time for her to talk on the phone, play with her computer and walk the dog." He grinned at me as if to say, "Did that help?"

***

It was nine o'clock that night when I finally dragged my weary bones into the family room.

"Whew!" I said in a voice just loud enough to wake my husband. "I'm tired out tonight."

Hubby opened his eyes. "Me too," he said, "and I'm hungry. Do we have anything to snack on?"

"You're in luck--I went to the grocery store today. Oh, I dropped your blue suit off at the dry cleaners, too; it will be ready tomorrow."

"Could you pick it up for me?" hubby said. "I won't have time."

"I guess. I have to drive Shane to his piano lesson and Erin to her dental appointment, but if the traffic isn't too heavy and I hit every green light I'll have time."

"Great."

"Before I forget," I said, "Erin's Brownie leader called a while ago. She wants to know if you would drive a carload of Brownies to the fire station on Saturday."

"Gee," my husband said, "I'd like to, honey, but I have work to do in the garage. Could you go instead?"

"Maybe," I said. "If I leave early enough to take Shane to the pool for his swimming lesson and get back in time to bake something for the church bazaar in the afternoon..."

Hubby smiled. "Thanks, dear; that will give me a chance to organize my nail collection."

"Don't mention it. I have to take the dog to the vet for her needle, make a dress to wear to Shane's piano recital on Monday and sort through last month's checks to find out why we don't balance with the bank statement, but I suppose I can squeeze in a trip to the fire station."

"Great."

I curled up on the couch and was almost asleep when I heard my husband's voice again.

"I forgot to tell you, dear; George called today. You remember George."

"Is he the one who wears lampshades on his head and sings Italian opera in an off-key Baritone?"

"He's the one," said hubby. "He's coming to town for a convention with his wife and kids and they want to stay here."

"Here? You don't mean here, as in this house?"

"What a kidder you are," said my husband. "Of course I mean here. Their plane lands tomorrow morning at ten. I told George you'll meet them at the airport. That's not a problem, is it?"

"Not for me, it isn't," I said. "I won't be here tomorrow; I'm trading places with Erin."

I'LL BE READY FOR HALLOWEEN THIS YEAR

Ever since I was born, three weeks late, I've been a procrastinator. I never do today the things I can put off doing until tomorrow.

For example, I don't mail the warranty card to the manufacturing company when I buy something new; I mean to—I just never get around to it.

I have warranty cards for my toaster that toasted its last bagel in 1999, for the first power saw I gave to my husband (he's now on his 8th), and for the electric train we gave our son for Christmas 1988—the train would only run around the track backwards and that novelty wore off in early 1989.

I never take the time to do things I know should be done, and I've recently decided that this is not a great way for me to go through life.

I want to change. I want to buy Christmas gifts before Dec 24th, I want to replace the empty toothpaste tube before my children's teeth turn yellow, I want to mail out birthday cards instead of "Sorry, I forgot" cards, and this year I want to be ready for Halloween.

I don't want to repeat the disasters of previous years.

Two years ago we spent Halloween at my mother's house.

We arrived just before supper. My husband and I were exhausted from the four-hour drive; Shane and Erin were excited.

They had seen little trick-or-treaters making the rounds before dark—miniature supermen in red capes and tights, fluffy white bunnies with pink noses and long black whiskers, and glittering Cinderella girls in layer after layer of hand-stitched ball gowns.

I knew I was in deep trouble.

"What are Shane and I going to be, Mom?" Erin's voice was eager.

"I want to be Dracula," said my son. "I'll wear black clothes and a long black cape. I'll paint my face green and I'll wear a set of plastic fangs like the ones I saw last week in the store. Remember, Mom--I asked if we could buy them and you said 'later'?"

I remembered.

"I'm going to be a scarecrow," Erin said. "I'll have hundreds of patches on my clothes and I'll wear a big straw hat with a yellow wig made out of yarn. Remember, Mom--last year you said I could be a scarecrow this year?"

I remembered.

My children did go trick or treating that night.

Shane wore granny glasses, a black velvet hat complete with a feather plume, and a purple shawl wrapped around his shoulders—a far cry from Dracula but a very good-looking fancy detective-type person.

Erin wore a man's striped blazer and an orange and green paisley tie and she sported a moustache drawn in wild abandon with my eyebrow pencil. She didn't have a yellow wig, but she did wear my grandfather's Derby hat.

I should have learned my lesson from that nightmare, but I'm thick-headed.

Last year my son telephoned from school to say that his class Halloween party was at two o'clock. I glanced at my watch—it was one-ten.

I had less than an hour to put together his costume, whip up a batch of Chocolate Goblin cookies for the party, pick up sodas at the corner store and deliver the whole thing to the school.

"By the way," my son added before he hung up, "Erin needs her costume, too."

I gave myself a good tongue-lashing while I stirred the cookie mixture until it boiled, and while I spooned the hot cookie mounds onto a sheet of waxed paper to cool, and while I hunted for the Little-Bo-Peep costume from Erin's figure skating show last spring.

I scavenged through my husband's closet and found a navy sports jacket and I borrowed "medals" from his Lions Club vest.

I grabbed gold rickrack from my sewing kit, red nail polish from my make-up bag and the blow dryer from its hook in the bathroom.

Shane would be a General—a wounded General.

I splattered the nail polish in big red gobs on the front of the jacket and blasted it with the hair dryer.

I pinned medals to the chest pockets and glued rickrack to the shoulders, then ran upstairs to find the wooden sword I knew Shane had in his room somewhere…

Thankfully, everything turned out okay.

I arrived at the school just in time for my children to get dressed in their costumes.

Little-Bo-Peep was minus her staff, the General's blood wasn't quite dried, and the Chocolate Goblins were a little warm, but no one seemed to mind, and the children enjoyed their parties.

But I was still shaking when I returned home.

I've got to change my ways, I thought.

***

Well, another Halloween is just around the corner. I will procrastinate no longer.

I'm going to ask Shane and Erin what they would like to be and I'll organize their costumes down to the last set of fangs.

On Halloween I'll sit back and smile at the compliments from friends and neighbors.

"Magnificent!" they'll say. "Wondrous! Look at the work you put into those costumes. What a good mother you must be."

Mothers everywhere will be proud of me; my own mother will be proud.

Yes, this Halloween I plan to have things in control. I'll know what characters my children will be, I'll know where to buy the patterns for their costumes, I'll know what kind of material I'll use to sew the outfits and I'll know exactly what accessories they'll need to complete their elaborate ensembles.

I'm going to start soon.

In fact, I'm going to write everything down on a list of "things to do".

I'll put "Halloween Costumes" near the top of the list, too—right under "mail the warranty card for the electric frying pan I bought six months ago".

I'll get started on that tomorrow.

HOME FOR THE HOLIDAYS

Home for the Holidays: these words make me think of snow-covered fields, crackling logs in a fireplace, red velvet dresses trimmed in ecru lace, and an extended family singing carols around an eight-foot tall Christmas tree--scenes from Currier & Ives prints.

When I was a child, Christmas was a community affair involving aunts, uncles, cousins, and maternal and paternal grandparents.

Every year an assortment of relatives gathered at my parents' large farmhouse to share a holiday meal, and their loud voices and laughter drifted through the farmhouse rooms.

We decorated the house with silver garlands and beaded ropes draped across wall pictures and mirrors, and we strung crepe-paper streamers woven into box-type links from room corners to ceiling lights.

We hung Christmas cards from doorways and added spruce boughs to the front staircase.

Christmas candy, Christmas peace and Christmas hugs were offered to one and all.

The days between Christmas and New Years were spent 'tree visiting'.

My family walked or drove from home to home, visiting relatives and neighbors, admiring their decorated trees and the gifts underneath them.

Every gift was hauled out from beneath the tree and explained--Susan got this lovely sweater from her grandmother--Deborah really needed new skates this year; her feet have grown so much just since September--sweet Mrs. Henderson from next door dropped off this box of delicious chocolates for the family...

Visits were kept short--the adults sipped eggnog, the children played with Christmas toys, everyone nibbled on sweets passed around on glass trays, and then we moved on to visit the next family.

Visitors dropped in to see our tree, too.

Our trees always looked nice after they was decorated, even though they started out with so many bare spots on their trunks that my father drilled holes in them and stuck in branches he had snipped from another tree for just such an emergency.

I'm not sure why we didn't drag a fuller tree home from the woods in the first place--maybe Dad liked a challenge, or maybe he liked to feel that he played a really important part in the Christmas tree ritual, or maybe he just wasn't any good at picking out trees.

However, when our gangly, scrawny tree was covered with lights, tinsel, icicles, ornaments, and cards it looked fine, especially at night, when you couldn't see it too clearly.

Christmas baking always began long before Christmas day.

My mother filled earthenware crocks with gumdrop cakes, aromatic light and dark fruitcakes wrapped in aluminum foil, and war cake made from her mother's favorite recipe.

She baked pan after pan of fancy squares and sheet after sheet of cookies that she then iced and decorated.

She pushed chunks of meat through a grinder, added spices, suet and fruit and filled pie shells with the sweet, spicy mincemeat mixture.

On Christmas Eve day she made pumpkin pies-- stirring eggs, cream, spices, honey and sugar into mashed pumpkin until it tasted just right, and then pouring the lick-the-bowl-clean filling into at least four empty pastry shells.

Pumpkin pie was a family favorite in our home and four pies might be just enough to see us through Christmas day!

On Christmas Eve the first piece of pumpkin pie was cut and placed on a plate--apparently that's what Santa liked to eat when he came to our home in the middle of the night.

On Christmas morning only crumbs of crust remained to say that Santa had found us, all right.

My father always looked disappointed--pumpkin pie was really his favorite treat, he said, and every year he hoped that Santa would leave a small bite behind for him, but that never happened.

Dad said if Santa had the first piece of pie then surely he deserved the second piece, and of course we children thought we deserved the third through sixth, so we all enjoyed pumpkin pie for breakfast on Christmas morning.

Even Mom had a piece of pie for breakfast on Christmas day, although I'm sure it went against her philosophy that we should all eat oatmeal for breakfast in the winter because it would stick to our ribs and help keep us warm.

After I grew up I realized that my family didn't have much money when I was a child, and that Christmas must have been stressful for my parents.

I don't remember understanding the impact of that as a child, though.

I knew that my cousins received many more gifts from Santa than we did at our house, and their gifts were usually more elaborate, too--electric trains and talking dolls and one-thousand-piece construction sets, but somehow that didn't seem to matter to me. I truly remember being happy with the gifts we did receive, even if there weren't many of them and they weren't expensive.

A Christmas I remember as being one of the best ever was the year my brothers, sister and I received a portable record player.

I don't recall what else I got that year, other than a record or two to play on the machine; maybe I didn't get much else at all, but just imagine--a record player!

We figured we had to be the best-loved children in the neighborhood.

Who cared if our cousins got a huge floor stereo that year--we could carry our record player from room to room if we wanted--take it up to our bedrooms if we wanted--surely that was better than owning a heavy floor model machine that had to stay in one place?

I've told my parents they shouldn't have felt bad about the Christmases they provided; they did the best they could and without realizing it at the time, they probably did me a favor.

I may not remember too many of the Christmas gifts I received as a child but I clearly remember what was important to me about Christmas.

I remember being surrounded by family and good friends; I remember being hugged by aunts and uncles; I remember the voices of my mother and her sisters trying to out-talk each other while the men laughed at them; and I remember the peaceful feeling that filled me Christmas nights when I sat in the darkened living room, staring at the tree lights, watching the universe twinkle in front of me.

These things I remember.

I sometimes wish that my two children could experience a Christmas like the ones I knew as a child, but that's impossible.

Circumstances change. Families change.

My parents divorced after their children grew up. My father remarried and spends Christmas holidays with his wife's family.

My siblings are spread from coast to coast and I haven't lived in my home town for twenty years.

My children don't know what it's like to be surrounded by an extended family of aunts, uncles and cousins.

My husband's job requires us to move every few years and we've never lived in a town close enough to any of our relatives to make it possible to 'tree visit' the way I remember doing as a child.

Christmas has definitely changed.

Cocooning is the catch-phrase now; we have small nuclear families spending private time behind locked doors. I doubt that many people picture Currier & Ives scenes when they hear the words *Home for the Holidays.*

What does all this mean? Does it mean today's families have given up on traditions? Does it mean we no longer value what we treasured as children?

I don't believe so; maybe we've altered traditions, but we haven't destroyed them.

Every December my children go with their dad to a Christmas tree farm or mall parking lot and pick out a tree.

After they bring it home and we declare it to be the best spindly, scrawny tree we've ever had, we set it up in the family room, then sit for hours, stringing together garland after garland of cranberries and popped corn while we watch a Christmas movie.

I continue with some of the baking traditions I learned from my mother; I bake gumdrop cakes and scotch cookies and pumpkin pies (using her recipes for everything), but I've replaced fruit cakes and mincemeat fillings with dill dips and cheese logs served with crackers and crunchy vegetables.

For supper on Christmas Eve we eat Shepherd's Pie, then the children open one gift each, set out a snack for Mr. Santa (a homemade cinnamon bun--my husband's favorite treat), and hang up personalized crocheted stockings before heading upstairs to bed.

Santa must always be hungry when he reaches our home in the middle of the night because only dried cinnamon crumbs remain on the plate in the morning.

For Christmas breakfast, because of course if Santa deserves the first cinnamon bun then my husband figures he deserves the second and the children and I figure we deserve the third through fifth, we eat warm, home-made cinnamon buns off china plates, wash the sweet, spicy bites down with orange juice in crystal goblets, and wipe the sugar granules off our chins with linen napkins.

Christmas night, after our bellies are filled and the dishes are done and the gifts are rearranged under the tree once again, we turn off all the lights in the family room except for the mini-lights on the tree, then sit in the near dark and watch the universe twinkling in front of us.

I shut my eyes, and for a moment I am a child again, hearing and smelling and seeing Christmas the way it was over thirty years ago.

I wonder what the phrase, *Home for the Holidays* will mean to my children when they're grown?

I can't guarantee they'll follow any of our holiday traditions once they're on their own, but while they're still young I can ensure they know what traditions are by not changing so much as a crumb of cinnamon sugar or a kernel of popped corn from Christmas to Christmas.

Circumstances change. Families change. I know that.

I know that necessity may force the next generation to alter traditions again, but maybe, just maybe, when my children sit in front of twinkling tree lights with children of their own beside them, they'll shut their eyes for a moment and will hear and smell and see Christmas the way it was for them twenty or thirty years before.

Maybe once again they'll smell cinnamon buns warm from the oven, will hear the clinking together of crystal goblets filled with orange juice, and will remember, like their mother before them, what was important about being *Home for the Holidays.*

OVERCOMING ENVY

Have you ever wanted something you knew you could never have? Ever envied someone who had exactly that one thing you'd trade your soul for? You have?

Me too, and that's why I think you'll be interested in my little story of sin and redemption.

I confess that for more years than I care to admit, I had an unladylike envy of a man's...beard.

It's true. No matter how hard I tried to be discreet about my attraction, no matter how determined I was not to stare when I saw a particularly long, thick one, I could never control myself.

Every time the opportunity arose I brushed up against bearded strangers in crowded malls and buses, or exclaimed to a surprised bearded man behind me at the grocery checkout, "Wow, what a great one! I wish I had one of those," or followed strange men on the street just to admire the way their beards jiggled when they sashayed down the sidewalk.

Not the actions of a well-adjusted woman.

Deep down I suspected that I couldn't have what I wanted. Deep down I realized it was socially unacceptable, as well as physically near-to-impossible for me to grow a beard. I just wished it wasn't so.

I had a good reason for feeling that way, too, for coveting a face-cover.

You see, I have no chin. Oh, I don't mean I have NO chin, in that my bottom teeth rest on my neck; I mean I don't have a proper, sticky-out chin--one to add length to my round face and provide me with a profile with which to be proud.

I was tired of providing entertainment at parties by imitating the man-in-the-moon--why couldn't I use a beard to cover my facial flaws? That's what men used them for. It wasn't fair.

Arnold is a prime example. He's an attractive man, so debonair in his red goatee.

"Consider it my finest asset," he says, and he grooms it with the pride of a doting parent. Who would guess that Arnold hides a receding chin under that red armor?

It's true; I sneaked a peek at his high school yearbook when I was visiting him one day, and there he was--beardless and chinless.

Fortunately for Arnold, I'm good at keeping secrets.

Then of course there's Ron, one of our local doctors, whose gray hair and gray-flecked beard gave him a real Kenny Rogers appeal, made him the heartthrob of every woman in town.

Did anyone care that he's forty pounds overweight, is nearing sixty, and has had a devoted wife (with a perfectly good chin, might I add), for thirty-five years? No.

Unfortunately for Dr. Ron he made the mistake last month of appearing in public sans gray-flecks. Not a single woman swooned over him; overnight he was transformed into just another old married man with a weight problem.

I heard from a reliable source that the good doctor regrets his decision to face life without a beard but is too embarrassed to re-grow it, afraid that townsfolk will consider him vain. Our town has its share of gossips and they like to talk about such things. That's what I heard, anyway.

I swear by the hair on my grandfather's chin, these are not isolated cases. Look around you--chin-whiskered men are everywhere. Are these males too cheap to buy electric razors, too timid to put steel blade to skin? I think not. Vanity, thy name is man.

My therapist (who by the way, has a perfectly good Sigmund Freud beard), said I had to get over my preoccupation with beards or risk it becoming an obsession.

"Do something constructive to confront your envious emotions," he said. "Perhaps pencil in beards on several of your old photos."

I figured any advice that cost me $100 a session must be good advice, so I did as he suggested.

My husband was a little upset when he found the altered snapshots, but I told him we had more wedding photos somewhere. (We didn't, as it turned out, but that's another story for another time.)

The good news is I've made a few startling revelations: I discovered that a beard isn't all its brushed up to be, I discovered that some people don't look good in beards, and I discovered there are worse things in life than having no chin--for example the very real possibility of me having no husband if I can't erase the beards from our pictures.

I have seen the light. I no longer desire a beard. I no longer want what I know I can never have.

I will now face the world as a well-adjusted, chinless woman, resorting to tricks of illusion to add length to my pie-plate face.

I have decided to wear dangling earrings that rest on my shoulder blades, avoid bowl-type hairstyles, always steer clear of turtlenecks, and wear my blouses open as low as decency and the law allows.

I'm even developing a new line of specialty clothing, due to hit the marketplace next spring, or maybe fall.

I have a gut-level feeling that after my line appears in the stores, beards will be out; *Clothes for the Chinless* will be in. I'm almost certain.

Is anyone ready to place an order?

TOKENS OF UNDYING LOVE

I house-cleaned my bedroom closet yesterday, and I was ruthless.

I filled a garbage-bag with bell-bottomed blue jeans, a green-striped, two-piece dress I've kept since 1975 (hoping its style would return to fashion-favor), and three pairs of high-heeled shoes I've been unable to wear since my knee operation four years ago.

I tossed out nightgowns that had only a few frayed seams, blouses I could still wear as long as I kept the collars and cuffs hidden, and a variety of purses that had straps missing, holes in their sides, and mildewed linings.

I was very proud of myself; I had only the right-hand side of my top shelf to tackle, and then I would start on my husband's closet.

I could really be ruthless with his things!

Reaching up to the shelf, I pulled down a chocolate box tied with a wrinkled ribbon.

My best intentions suddenly dissipated into the wintry air and I couldn't resist the urge to peek inside the box.

So I sat on my bed, untied the ribbon bow, and removed the cover.

There they were—yellowed letters and faded valentines; I'd all but forgotten I had them.

Maybe it was time to throw them out. Surely these bits of paper from my past had no meaning in my life now.

I fingered a packet of letters dated 1969. 1969--so long ago!

I opened one envelope and read the words written in a familiar hen-scratching; penmanship was never one of my husband's strong points.

Suddenly I was sixteen again, and in love, full of dreams about the future with my knight-in-shining-armor, a knight-in-shining-armor who was spending the summer at an Air Cadet Camp in Quebec.

I waited for the mail car to arrive every day at noon. When letters arrived I was ecstatic, and in my bedroom I read them over and over and over again.

The letters promised undying love from a lanky, fuzzy-cheeked boy, to me, a skinny, hair-to-the-waist dreamer.

Undying love! What did two teenagers know about undying love?

Undying love meant I wanted to spend all my time either talking to my loved one or about him, or wishing I was talking to him or about him.

It meant I wrote our initials in red ink on the back of my scribblers, on the front of my scribblers and in tiny hearts on my pencil case.

It meant I worried about the way I looked, about the way I dressed and about whether or not my breath was fresh.

Undying love meant I was insecure enough to be jealous of every other girl who came in contact with my chosen one--surely he would realize that someone else was a better match for him than I was, and he would dump me.

I picked up a faded valentine—a pale red heart with ecru doily lace around the edges and "All My Love Forever," printed on the back.

I loved Valentine's Day when I was a teenager.

Valentine's Day meant chocolates in heart-shaped boxes, or maybe a gift of dime-store earrings, or a date to an Annette Funicello-Frankie Avalon movie.

Valentine's Day meant LOVE.

I looked up from my dreaming.

Valentine's Day! That's right, it was coming soon. I knew, because I had to bake eight dozen heart-shaped cookies for my children's school parties.

I had to help my daughter tear thirty-two valentines plus one for her teacher out of a Valentine's Day book, and I had to help my son find enough valentines without any hugs, kisses, or yucky, mushy words on them to give to the girls in his class.

Hopefully I would even find the time and energy to have a quiet Valentine's Day supper with my husband after we tucked the children into bed that night.

I pulled out more valentines and letters from the box and spent an hour reminiscing.

Funny thing how life turns out, how a knight-in-shining-armor becomes a businessman in a three-piece suit, and a hair-to-the-waist dreamer becomes a grey-haired, always-on-the-go mother of two children.

Even the term, 'undying love' has changed in meaning to me.

Now, undying love means my husband brings me a cup of coffee in bed on a Sunday morning.

It means I share the newspaper with him at the lunch table and we trade bits of interesting articles out loud.

It means when I have a headache or the flu I can lie down and know my chosen one will put the children to bed with a story and a hug.

Undying love means we kiss each other good-bye in the mornings and good-night before we sleep.

It means I know exactly what size socks, shirts and shoes to buy my husband, and it means he knows not to buy ANY of my clothes.

It means we split the last piece of pizza, even though we'd each like to eat the whole thing.

It means we've shared the heartache of family divorce, and death, and have cried on each other's shoulders.

Undying love means we don't make cruel remarks about each other's parents and siblings.

It means I don't tell my husband he has gained weight, and he doesn't compare my cooking to his mother's.

It means I look at this nearing-middle-age, responsible man and see a lanky, fuzzy-cheeked boy lurking just beneath the surface.

I heard the school bus stop at the end of our driveway.

"Mom, we're home!"

I quickly tucked the valentines and letters back into the chocolate box and retied the frayed ribbon, then stood on tiptoe and pushed the box back into the far corner of my closet shelf.

I turned to leave the room, changed my mind, and instead bent to retrieve my green-striped, two-piece dress from the garbage.

After all, there is such a thing as being too ruthless!

DO YOU WORK?

It's snowing again today; the weather office predicts twenty centimeters of the white stuff for our area.

The schools didn't even try to open--I'm sure that the administrators realized it would be a waste of time and money; the buses would barely have time to drop the children off at school before they'd have to begin the return trips home because of heavy snow, slippery roads, and zero visibility.

Days like this I'm glad I don't work outside the home. If I did I'd have to take a vacation day or find a sitter willing to brave the elements and drive to my place to look after my children.

When I was first married I worked for an insurance company, but then we started moving every year or so because of my husband's career and it became difficult for me to find employment in new towns or cities, depending on the job market at the time.

When our children were born my husband and I decided that I would stay home with them; we agreed that looking after our two children was full-time work, at least while they were preschoolers.

So I spent a lot of time with them--we made crafts, went to story-times at the library, met with other mothers and their preschoolers for play dates, built Lego castles and Barbie car garages and read stories.

The years flew by.

Even after Shane and then Erin started school I kept busy all day, and after school I became the chauffeur, ferrying my children to piano and swimming lessons, Brownies and Cubs, skating rinks and sledding hills.

The children like the fact that I'm home when they arrive at the door after the bus drops them off, that I can sit and cuddle with them when they're too sick to go to school, and that I'm home when school is cancelled due to a storm or a teacher-conference day.

Not that I'm always here, mind you.

I go out, buy the groceries, run all the errands that need to be done, pay the bills, go to the library for writing research and do a lot of traipsing around the city to ensure our family unit runs along with as few bumps as possible, but most of the time I'm home when the children need me.

I've run various part-time jobs from my home over the years: I've pushed Shane in the stroller while going door to door as a local Avon representative, I've sold plant-growing systems via the house-party route, and I've taken over the dining room table to teach a variety of crafts to interested women, but none of these occupations were particularly lucrative.

Some days I'm filled with guilt because I don't contribute much to the family income.

There are times when we run a bit short of money, or times when we would like to buy something but know we can't afford it, or times when my husband and I are both tired and stressed.

That's when I worry that I'm wasting my life by staying at home, and on those days I have to remind myself that I'm playing an important role in the raising of our children.

I know that large numbers of children are being looked after in day care centers these days, and sometimes I wonder if those experiences will affect their outlooks on life when they are adults.

Wiil they believe that financial security is more essential than emotional security, that work is more important than family, that children have only themselves to rely on because most times there's not another soul around who loves them the way their parents do and is there for them when they really need a hug or a snuggle or a reassuring word?

I'm not implying that my children will grow up without their own worries and problems. I'm sure they will. But for now I'm doing what my husband and I feel is best for our family.

Maybe that's all any of us can do--the best we can.

It's not up to me to judge what other parents choose to do or need to do; I only ask that I not be judged, either.

When I'm at parties or social functions with my husband I'm often asked, "Do you work?"

If I reply, "No," the person who asked nods his or her head and turns away to find a more interesting soul.

If I reply, "Not at a regular job, no, but I do work," the person says, "Oh, I realize that looking after a house is work, of course," and then they turn away to find a more interesting soul.

I'm tempted to say, "Yes, I work. Thank you for asking. Do you work?"

And then, no matter what the reply, even if the man says he's a scientist who is just about to release the cure for the common cold, or the woman says she works for CIA covert operations, I'll nod my head and then turn away as if to search for a more interesting soul in the room.

Sometimes I reply, "I'm a writer."

This response usually draws a blank look from the person who asked the question and then after a few seconds he or she will say, "A writer--isn't that nice. What do you write?"

"Oh, the usual," I say. "You know: letters, grocery lists, checks to the tax man, Christmas card notes--important stuff."

This answer is great because I'm then usually branded a 'crazy person' and am not bothered again with any stupid conversations for the rest of the evening.

The only downside to this approach is that the guests begin to give my husband sympathetic looks, as if he's a puppy in an animal shelter, and then he feels compelled to quiz me about my conversations with Harry Dean or Mary Stone.

When he asks me I just shrug my shoulders and pretend I don't know what on earth would make them start acting weird around him--did he remember to wear deodorant tonight? Did he have meatball sauce on his tie? Was his zipper unzipped?

I'm hopeful that if my husband ever did discover the truth he would understand; he knows I have a warped sense of humor and yet he married me anyway, and he knows that I become frustrated by people who decide to write me off as not being an interesting person simply because I don't head out the door in a suit every day on my way up a corporate ladder.

I imagine that one day I will seek gainful employment again, probably once Shane and Erin complete elementary school, but that won't be for a few more years.

Until then, I'll enjoy the snow days with my children and will cherish the memories we're creating together as a family.

I have to go for now, though--Shane and Erin are outside building a snow man and they need a hat, a scarf and a carrot nose to complete their masterpiece.

I'm sure my husband won't mind if I lend Frosty one of his ties, too, in case he decides to look for work while he's here this winter.

The purple and orange tie my mother-in-law gave hubby for Christmas last year would be perfect, I think. Yes, the perfect touch.

"Shane! Erin! Look what I have for your snowman!"

GOING HOME

You can never go home again.

The majority of adults have probably heard that phrase tossed about a few times, and some adults might even believe those words to be true, but I don't.

I admit I can't physically return to my childhood home; that home has changed owners several times since my days of childhood.

I admit too, that even if I could physically return 'home', it wouldn't be the same place I remember; playmates have grown up, adults have grown old, and grandparents have died.

I can go back to visit in my 'mind's eye', though, and those visits are filled not only with tangible images I could describe to you, such as trees and barns and gardens, but just as importantly with intangible things, such as the smell of fresh-cut hay, the crackle of ice beneath skate blades and the laughter of children on a summer afternoon.

***

I shimmy up the giant maple tree in the front yard, climb high in its branches, sit on the wooden seat my older cousin fastened there, and stare for hours at the world below.

At the end of the driveway my brothers are scooping polliwogs out of the ditch to transfer to their special 'polliwog hole' in the back yard. My younger brother walks as if his rubber boots are filled with water, which they are.

***

I wave to my cousins from next door. They're in the field that separates our houses, and they fight over who should get the higher of the two swings. I join them, and we take turns pushing each other up, up, up in the air. As each push sends me higher and higher, I hold my breath, certain that the very next push will be the one that sends me over the top of the support poles, but that never happens. I descend each time toward the ground again and laugh out loud.

***

Now my father burns the grass, preparing for summer. The smoke-smell is earthy, like the piles of leaves I jumped into last fall. I breathe in a big breath, and my eyes water. We children gather around the fringe of the fire like holiday campers at a cook-out.

"You're it." My brother taps me on the arm and runs.

"Away from the fire, children," our father warns, and our game of tag is moved to the back field until one of the adults remembers it's a school night and calls us inside for bed.

***

"Corn-on-the-cob for supper tonight, girls," my mother says, and hands my sister and me a large pot. "Make sure the cobs are filled-out."

On the way to the corn rows I pick a few peas, shell them quickly into my mouth, munching their juicy sweetness, and throw the empty pods into the field so my mother won't know about my pre-dinner snack.

The late afternoon sun is hot, so my sister and I quickly fill the pot with the sweetest corn in the world.

At supper I crunch my way through eight golden cobs and wear a butter-grin on my face.

***

It's Sunday afternoon; church has finished, lunch is over, and relatives from town have arrived for a visit.

My 'town' cousins watch, fascinated, as my father milks the cow.

"Know how we get cream?" my father says, his blue eyes twinkling.

"How?" Curious cousins take the bait.

"You have to pump the cow's tail—that turns the milk into cream."

Wide-eyed cousins dutifully take turns pumping Bossy's tail while my father chuckles and encourages them, "Faster, faster."

***

I'm in the barn with my sister and brothers.

"Last one up is a rotten egg," my sister shouts.

One after another we scramble up the wooden ladder to the overhead loft, stepping over and around holes in the floorboards until we're crouched at the edge of the loft, peering down.

On the barn floor below lays a pile of loose hay, just waiting for us, just begging us to take the plunge and dive into it.

Arms flapping and hair flying, we throw ourselves into the air and land with a soft "oomph". Then it's a race to get back up the ladder again for another jump.

***

The stilts my father made are high, so high we have to stand on my mother's clothesline step to climb onto them.

Off we go like circus performers, wobbling down the lane. My older brother is "King of the Stilts", and always walks the farthest before toppling to the ground.

Then back we go to the clothesline step, giggling and laughing and arguing about who went the fastest and whose stilts are highest and who will someday walk on stilts taller than the seat in our maple tree.

***

"How about a hug?" my grandfather says.

He rubs his chin back and forth against my tender cheeks, and his snow-white whisker-stubble burns my face.

I pull away.

"Sorry about that," he says. "Why don't you give me a whisker-rub back?" and I try, even though I know what will happen.

Sure enough, when I rub my chin back and forth against my grandfather's rough cheeks, my skin burns again.

"Hedley, stop teasing the child," my grandmother says, and my grandfather laughs at his own wickedness.

***

"Red rover, red rover, send Sylvia right over!"

Our game ends when the teacher rings her hand bell, and the rag-tag collection of children comprising grades one to six line up, girls in one line and boys in another, to head into the one-room schoolhouse to start the day.

I swallow my cod-liver-oil capsule without biting it like the boys do, and wash it down with a drink of water from my red collapsible drinking cup I filled at the fountain in the hallway.

At recess we pick up the game of Red Rover again, or play flies-and-grounders or hopscotch or marbles until it's time to head back into the classroom.

***

"Sylvia, will you go down to the cellar and get potatoes for supper? And we need a jar of pickles, too," Mom says.

She hands me a bag to put the potatoes in and I grudgingly head to the cellar stairs.

I don't like the cellar in our farmhouse; I think it's smelly and damp and full of spiders and monsters that eat little children.

But I know that when my mother asks me to go down there she is really telling me to go down there and I have no choice but to 'go down there', so I go, slowly and carefully, down the cement steps.

I open the creaky wooden door at the bottom of the steps and pull a chain to turn on an overhead light bulb. Already I'm nervous about what might be lurking in the shadows.

The potatoes are kept in a 'cold room', in an open bin along the side of the wall.

One of the things I hate about potatoes in the cellar is that parts of them keep on growing while they are there; they sprout long spindly tentacles that feel like giant spider legs when I reach for them.

Sometimes my brothers and I have to go down to the cold room and remove all the sprouts from the potatoes and not one of us likes that job.

But today I just have to reach in and pick out enough of the tubers to fill the bag, so I do it as quickly as I can, before the monsters know I'm there.

Then I head to where the pickles and other canned goods are kept, at the FAR end of the cellar, past the two furnaces that gurgle and groan, past the odds and ends that my parents have stored there in case they need them sometime, and up a slight incline to where the preserves are kept on wooden shelves.

I find sweet-mixed pickles, dill pickles, pickled beets and green tomato chow. I'm not sure which kind of pickles mom wants for supper so I grab a bottle of dill and a bottle of sweet-mixed and practically run all the way back to the wooden door.

I only breathe a sigh of relief when I finally turn off the light and shut the door behind me.

I'm safe one more time.

***

Mom is making doughnuts today and I'm allowed to help.

I watch as she prepares the batter and heats the fat and cuts the doughnut shapes out of the dough.

My job comes after the doughnuts are deep-fried a golden brown; I place the warm doughnuts into a brown paper bag with white sugar in it, and shake the bag like a maraca until the doughnuts are covered in a coating of sweetness.

Mom doesn't waste anything; she cooks the 'doughnut holes' after the doughnuts are finished, and my siblings and I get to eat some of them right then and there, while they are still warm. That is a special treat we all enjoy and we lick the sugar off our fingers.

***

My childhood ended years ago, but by taking the time to reminisce, to *Go Home*, I can once again feel the breeze on my face as my swing soars up to touch the sun, can hear my sister's girlish whisper in the dark of night assuring me there's nothing hiding in my closet, can smell and touch and see my childhood world as clearly as if I was still up in my maple tree looking down.

How about you? Have you gone home lately?

LIFE WITH A COLICKY KID

No matter what the experts say about all babies crying, I'll go to my grave swearing that while all babies may cry, some babies really CRY!

My first born, Shane, was a healthy baby who fussed when he needed something but was contented otherwise.

"What great parents we are." My husband and I congratulated each other. "We must do this again."

Our daughter, Erin, was born three years later.

The nurses at the hospital said, "What a lovely baby girl you have. She eats and sleeps, sleeps and eats; she's a perfect child."

We took our perfect child home, and six days later life as we knew it turned into a five-month-long nightmare. Our perfect child cried and cried and cried.

"This can't be happening," I said. "Second children aren't supposed to be colicky; there must be something wrong."

Our doctor examined Erin and could find no physical reason for her distress.

"Live with it," he said. "She'll outgrow it in a few months."

That was easy for him to say. He didn't spend his nights walking the floors, holding a screaming infant. He didn't have to function on two or three hours of sleep a night broken into half-hour chunks. He didn't try in vain to soothe an obviously miserable baby.

A good friend of mine lent me a rocking chair and I spent many nights in that chair, rocking, rocking, rocking with Erin crying in my lap or on my shoulder.

It was my crying baby and me against the world; at three o'clock in the morning everyone else in the entire universe slept except for us.

One night around four AM it finally dawned on me why Erin cried—she HATED ME, that was why! The rational part of me knew this wasn't true, but the dead-on-my-feet part of me could think of no other logical explanation.

My husband and I tried everything and anything to soothe our child. Walking, rocking, singing, noisy rooms, silent rooms, driving in the car, running the vacuum cleaner...nothing helped.

A trip to McDonalds' restaurant four kilometers from our house was a major undertaking. One day we made it halfway there but Erin was crying so hard that we decided to return home.

That turned out to be a bad decision on our part because our problem then escalated—Erin was crying because she always cried, but now Shane was crying because he liked McDonalds and really wanted to go there.

We finally turned the car around again and ordered our food at the drive-through. At least then we were back to having only one crying child in the backseat; Shane was smiling again and playing with the toy from his Happy Meal.

For several months I was consumed with guilt, sometimes because I thought my baby hated me, other times because I was afraid I would end up hating her. I was totally exhausted, a walking zombie. I didn't think I would ever catch up on the sleep I was missing.

Most nights it was six in the morning before Erin finally settled down for a nap after crying all night, and then I'd stumble into bed like a drunken sailor.

Around six-thirty I'd be awakened by three-year-old Shane tugging at my arm.

"What's for breakfast, Mom?" he'd say in his cheery, wide-awake, let's-set-the-world-on-fire voice.

Five months of my life passed in a blur.

My family did survive. By the age of one Erin progressed from being a colicky baby to being just plain fussy, and by the age of two she was what we called a fuss-budget, expecting perfection from herself and from life in general.

She's eleven years old now and in grade six. She is friendly and polite, has a wonderful sense of humor, and loves her parents and her brother. Her report cards are super, and her teachers always comment that she's a pleasure to have in class.

She still expects a lot from herself, and her feelings are easily bruised if she feels she doesn't measure up, but she's a great kid, and my husband and I wouldn't trade her for the world.

I sometimes wonder if my daughter was a colicky baby because she has supersensitive skin or perhaps has a sensitive digestive system. Or maybe it's simply the personality she was born with, something neither she nor I had any control over.

Maybe.

I'm just happy to report that she now sleeps through the night.

ONE MOTHER'S DAY

One Mother's Day in the early 1980s my husband and I decided to take our respective mothers out for a nice dinner. Of course we included our own little children in the outing–it was Mother's Day after all, a time for mothers and children to be together, enjoying each other's company.

The day started off great; the sun was shining and the gentle breeze was cool but not cold like it can be sometimes in early May.

Hubby and I dressed the children and packed the car for the trip.

Five and a half year old Shane was a cute little blond boy clad in a red T-shirt and pants, and not-quite three year old Erin was adorable in a blue dress I had smocked and sewn for her.

In fact, we all looked so nice that day that hubby took a picture of us once we arrived at my mom's place, before we picked up my mother-in-law and headed to the restaurant.

We chose a restaurant in a neighboring town; a Chinese food place, although I can't remember its name now.

We all loved Chinese food; even little Erin and Shane enjoyed egg rolls and rice and Chow Mein, so this was a perfect choice for a Mother's Day celebration.

The restaurant was busy when we arrived, but luckily we had remembered to call ahead for a reservation and our table was ready in no time at all. We ordered our food, poured wine for the adults (except for my husband's mom, who doesn't drink alcohol), and milk for the children.

Shane and Erin were very well behaved–they said 'please' and 'thank you' in all the right places, sat quietly until the meal arrived, and offered funny little comments throughout dinner that helped keep the mood light and the conversation flowing.

I was such a proud mom.

Finally we finished the meal; none of us could eat any more and all that was left to do was pay the bill and head home.

While hubby went to the counter to settle the tab, the two grandmothers, the children and I waited near the entrance.

Before I could say, "Shane, come back here", my cute little blond boy, dressed all in red, snuck up behind a woman who was having a quiet lunch with her adult daughter and yelled, "BOO" in his loudest voice ever!

The poor mother shrieked and dropped her fork while her daughter burst into gales of laughter. The other patrons in the restaurant stared, and I looked around for a hole into which I could crawl. Shane, in the meantime, smiled at everyone and walked back to join our little group as if nothing had happened.

Of course I insisted, as any good mother would, that he apologize to the lady that he frightened, and to his credit he did, but I'm not even certain the woman heard him over her daughter's continuous laughter.

"Funniest thing I've ever seen," the daughter said, wiping her eyes. "Happy Mother's Day, Mom, we'll have to come here again next year!"

I scanned the restaurant for my husband but he had already retreated to our car, so I ushered Shane and Erin outside and the two grandmothers trailed behind us, almost, but not quite, hiding their grins and stifling their laughter...

The next May we ordered take-out fried chicken and ate it with my mother at her home; it seemed like the best thing to do.

I often wonder, though, if that daughter took her mother back to that Chinese restaurant on Mother's Day the next year, and if she sat in the same seat, hoping that Shane would arrive for an encore performance.

LETTER TO SANTA

Dear Santa,

Just a quick note to remind you that Christmas is coming soon. I've been a busy elf for weeks already and I still have so much to do.

I haven't even finished my Christmas shopping—when I checked my list twice I discovered I'd forgotten all about dear Aunt Emily, my unmarried cousin Mortimer, and my mother-in-law.

I have to remedy that, Santa, because I simply adore dear Aunt Emily and Cousin Mortimer.

I also have Christmas cleaning to do; my husband likes the house to be tidy when he drags a needle-dropping tree and armloads of sticky spruce boughs through the back door, down the carpeted hallway and into the living room.

Ah, yes, Santa, having a living thing plucked out of the forest by folks eager to please me and take my money truly reflects the Christmas spirit.

My husband plunks the tree into a foil-covered bucket filled with sand. Such elegance! It will be absolutely perfect once it's decorated.

I free my one hundred and ninety-four hand-crafted Christmas ornaments from their tissue-paper cocoons.

Hand-made ornaments add a special touch, don't they, Santa?

The fact that I didn't make the ornaments doesn't bother me at all. I'm certain the workers in China put love into every plastic snowman and angel they produced. They certainly knew what they were doing, too; all the ornaments look the same—the average person would never believe they were made by hand.

I almost forgot about popping the corn. Stringing popcorn is a family tradition in my home, a special Christmas task that brings mother and children together.

Shane and Erin love to watch me fill several large mixing bowls with the exploded vegetable, then thread fishing line onto darning needles and tie knots at the end of the line so the popcorn doesn't slide right off onto the floor when they start to help with the job.

They do good work, too—usually managing to string a dozen kernels each before they bombard me with complaints about bleeding fingers. Of course they don't want to drip blood onto the popped corn kernels, so that's when they hand the bowls and strings and needles back to me to finish the task.

Considerate little elves, aren't they, Santa?

Last but not least, we decorate the top of the tree.

The children and I stare, spellbound, as my husband ever-so-gently adjusts the crowning glory—a plastic Rudolph face that has been handed down in my family for one generation. (Well, it WILL be one generation as soon as I hand it down once.) I found this treasure at a flea market last year for only twenty-five cents, and Rudy's nose even lights up!

Oh, before I forget, Santa, I want to mention that my children wrote to you last evening. They struggled with words such as "reindeer" and "exceptionally good", but I think you'll be able to decipher most of their ~~demands~~ requests.

They hope you'll forget about the time they took their grandma's false teeth out of the bathroom and tied both sets onto Mr. Teddy Bear, and they hope you weren't looking the day they threw snowballs at the local banker, and most of all, they hope you'll forgive them for selling my ten-speed bicycle and my husband's ride-on mower at our garage sale last fall. (I didn't even know we were HAVING a garage sale until the enterprising little tykes presented me with the profits--$15.42!)

I'm fortunate to have such adorable children, aren't I, Santa?

I remind myself of that every December as I compete with other mothers in the toy stores.

"I need that," I say politely as I grab a 'must-have' doll from a fellow shopper's hand and run with it to the cashier. "You'd better learn to hold on tighter, dearie."

"Drop it," I say to a woman who has a death-grip on the only 800-piece building set left in town. A well-placed bite on the hand punctuates my courteous smile, and I head to the cash counter a happy mother.

Yes, Santa, the Christmas season makes me realize how truly blessed I am; I have a loving family at my side and dear friends nearby.

The only way I could possibly feel even more blessed is if I'd get what I really want for Christmas.

Last night the children were writing their letters to you when my younger child turned to me and said, "Why don't you write Santa a letter, Mommy?"

What a good idea, I thought. *What should I ask for? I'm too old for paper dolls and I still have about seven hundred bricks left in my one thousand piece building set from last year. I've had more than my share of perfume, peanuts and panty hose. I don't need slippers, glass swans, or monogrammed serviettes, and if I live to be ninety-nine, I'll still have an ample supply of frying pans, fondue forks and fuzzy dice.*

So this year, Santa, I've decided to be grown up. I won't ask for toys. This year I'll present you with a list of things that an ordinary, run-of-the-mill, nearsighted, slightly overweight woman wants to have abolished. I'll keep my list simple--no sense suggesting the impossible, such as abolishing hatred, wars, famine or even school yard bullies.

No, this list will surely be within your power to fill.

For Christmas this year I would like you to please abolish the following:

- The words, "What do you do all day now that your children are in school?
- Christmas mail-order catalogues that arrive in the summer and summer catalogues that arrive in December.
- Television evangelists who ask for money from people who can least afford to give.
- Expensive 'Designer label' clothing for children.
- 'Wrong number' phone calls after midnight; I'm always positive that somebody dear to me has died and my heart can't take the stress anymore.
- The words, "I wasn't going to tell you this, but…"

- Washing machines that devour socks--it wouldn't be so bad if they ate matching pairs, but they prefer a diet of one brown and one blue or one blue and one white or one white and one yellow or…
- Fast food commercials that coerce my children into BEGGING to have junk food for supper.

That's about it, Santa; I would appreciate any help you can give me with the above list. And to assure you that I'm not trying to be greedy or too demanding I'm also including a list of things that are great just the way they are. You don't have to change a thing.

- Licorice all-sorts, baby dill pickles, smoked oysters.
- Sand in all our summer clothes--this means we've had a great time at the cottage.
- Babies falling asleep in my arms.
- White wine accompanying a late-night supper with my husband.
- The sound of waves crashing over rocks, crickets in a field, the cry of seagulls, night silence.
- Old friends who know most of my faults and love me anyway.
- The feeling of joy when my bank statement balances with my checkbook.
- Going to bed at two in the morning on Christmas Eve and getting up three hours later with the children to discover that "Santa had come, all right!"

I could also mention hot showers, cool breezes, toast with real butter and long walks on the beach with my husband, but I know that you have many other letters to read before you fill your sleigh with presents, so I will end here.

Have a nice Christmas. I've tried to be well-behaved all year--please overlook the July first weekend.

Sincerely,

Sylvia

P.S.

If you happen to have an extra package of paper dolls when you get to my house, I'd love one!

Happy Holidays!

FIRST WEEK OF SCHOOL

Ah yes, motherhood; dreams from a young girl's fancy.

I remember my own mother's reflections about how rewarding it was to be a mother--how life becomes fulfilled with the birth of a child.

"Best thing I ever did, bringing children into this world", she said. "My life would not have been complete without the pitter-patter of tiny toes and heels throughout my house."

Well, don't talk to me about fulfillment today.

How could any mother feel fulfilled after dealing with a crying five-year-old about to step out alone into the world of teachers, busses and school-yard bullies?

Fulfilled is the last emotion I feel right now. I'm scared, worried, concerned, and nervous. I worry that I'm a failure as a parent--I should have better prepared my child to face the outside world.

I'm filled with guilt because part of me looks forward to an entire day home alone, and I'm frustrated with my daughter because her socks, panties, sneakers, pants, and shirt "bother" her.

"They bother me," is her lament these days. She has worn the same pair of pants for three days in a row because her other clothes (hanging neatly and cleanly in her closet), "botherrrrr me," she says.

Forget about style. Forget about wearing anything that buttons or has elastic (it's either too tight or too loose), is too long (touches her ankle bones), is too short (doesn't touch her ankle bones), is a yucky color (varies from day to day), or has itchy seams (all seams are itchy to Erin).

Socks are out--it doesn't matter what color, size, shape or form they are--they're not right. They "bother" her toes, or they "bother" her heels, or they won't go up over her pant leg or they go too far up over her pant leg or (well, you get the picture).

I paw through the sock counter at the local department store like a stray cat digging through a garbage bin, hoping to find that elusive, perfect pair of socks. Anything that would stay on my daughter's feet for over five seconds would be treasured like gold!

But as hard as I've tried, so far I've been thwarted in my pursuit of the perfect pair of socks. The ones I've brought home have not been worth even a lump of coal.

My daughter hates every single pair.

Erin's timing, in matters of 'clothing crises', is impeccable.

She can be fully dressed, after many false starts, standing at the kitchen door with her lunch box in one hand and her pink book bag over her shoulders, ready for the day, when somehow, some way, she senses that the big yellow bus is making its approach to our driveway. It's at that very moment that she throws herself onto the kitchen floor, deftly pulls off her sneakers and socks, and slides her pant legs up to her knees faster than I can shout, "No!"

I'm left standing at the sidelines, unable to help, unable to cope. My mind reels as I think over and over again...I have twelve years of THIS to go through!

Several mornings Erin and I have both collapsed in tears, totally frustrated at this new level in our mother-daughter relationship.

Before the strict timetable-regime of school busses and teachers became our clock we had time to dress at a more leisurely pace. We could wait for favorite socks and pants to finish in the dryer if need be or completely ignore schedules if we so chose. That luxury for us, I'm afraid, has disappeared the way of the dinosaurs.

It saddens me to think that we're both being forced, against our wills, to conform to society's rules.

I realize that my small daughter is rebelling the only way she knows she has control over. I understand this. I accept it as a learning experience for us both. Deep down I know this stage in life won't last forever.

But...I'd still give anything to find my daughter a comfortable pair of socks!

DO NOT WALK ON THIS SURFACE

At the supermarket yesterday, when I reached into an open cooler for a package of frozen, no-name brand fish sticks, I noticed a warning printed on the white shelf.

Do Not Walk on This Surface, the warning stated in bold red letters.

Now hold on; did the store owners seriously think there was even a remote chance that I would somehow climb up onto their shelf? To do what--cavort? Dance?

This shelf was four feet above floor level; I would have to step on the frozen pizzas, work my way up through frozen Chinese food and mangle a few bags of frozen peas on my climb to the top. Not only would that be an admirable feat for someone who is only five feet three inches tall, twenty pounds overweight and not in the least inclined to be athletic, but I wouldn't even have been able to stand up if I had managed to scramble to that lofty height--the top of the cooler was barely twenty-four inches above the shelf!

But someone must have climbed onto that shelf at one time; otherwise why would the store feel compelled to issue a warning against any further infractions? Somewhere, sometime, somehow, shoppers must have defied the laws of science--space, gravity, etc--and climbed up on that high shelf to look down on the grocery-store world.

I eyed the general area of the meat department, looking for possible offenders. I spotted an elderly couple browsing through the bologna; surely they were potential suspects.

Oh--what about that woman with the toddler? She looked just the type to defy the law by placing her child bodily into the cooler and making him climb onto the shelf. I gave her a dirty look, to let her know I was keeping an eye on her.

She smiled at me. The nerve!

I decided to conduct a survey--question a few shoppers to see if anyone would admit to ever having committed this hideous crime against the store owners.

I strolled up to the shopper nearest me.

"And you, Father, have you ever committed the sin of walking on forbidden shelves?"

The priest looked at me serenely. "My child, we all sin and come short of the glory of God, but I don't believe I have ever committed that particular transgression."

"Thank you, Father; I was just checking."

So much for the theory that it is always the ones you least suspect.

I tried another route.

"Excuse me, ma'am," I began, "I'm conducting a survey and wondered if I could have a moment of your time."

"Speak up, dearie," the elderly woman replied, grabbing my arm. "My hearing isn't the best and I refuse to wear a hearing-aid. I hate them. My daughter, Bertha, shouted at me yesterday that it was high-time I give in and buy one, but like I said to my friend Rose, 'I'm not going to and that's final.' Rose agreed with me, too, although I had to tell her three times before she understood what I was saying. She's a little hard of hearing, you know."

It took me a good five minutes to extricate myself from the old lady's clutches, so when I did I pushed my shopping cart to the opposite end of the department.

One more attempt, then I had to leave; my children were due home from school soon.

I decided to choose my next suspect carefully; people were beginning to stare.

Aha! A man was hanging around the frozen food cooler. He was young, athletic-looking, and didn't have a shopping cart--a definite possibility.

I ducked around the corner and watched him for a minute. He did act suspiciously, bending down, then standing up, then bending down again.

I walked up to him. "Okay, buddy," I said, "tell me the truth--are you going to walk on that shelf?"

The young man put down his broom.

"Are you asking me to, lady?" he said. "It's against story policy, you know. I could get fired. If you can't reach something I'll get a step stool to help you," and he disappeared behind doors that read, 'Employees Only'.

I gave up and was about to leave the department when I noticed a store suggestion box in the corner.

'This Is Your Store', the sign above the box read. 'Tell Us How We Can Improve It.'

Management had even thoughtfully supplied a pad of paper and a pencil tied to a piece of string bolted onto the box.

I grabbed the pencil and wrote in fine print, neatly so they'd know I was serious.

If I am going to be told not to walk on a shelf I would at least like to be told not to walk on a shelf that is within my capabilities of walking on. May I suggest that in the future you place your signs on lower shelves so that even the most out-of-shape, non-athletic, over-the-hill shopper like me can have a chance to obey the warning? Thank you.

I felt much better after I finished writing that note, and my spirits were soaring as I neared the dairy case.

"Let's see now. I need sour cream, butter and strawberry yogurt."

I had to stretch to reach the sour cream; my nose and eyes barely cleared the shelf and I was standing on tiptoe.

Then my spirits suddenly wilted like last week's lettuce.

Do Not Walk on This Surface a sign warned.

I backed my cart into an inconspicuous corner, by the cheese slices, and scanned the area for possible suspects.

HONEY, WE'VE BEEN TRANSFERRED

I glanced at the kitchen clock. It was ten minutes before four on a Friday afternoon, that notorious time of the week many mobile families dread.

I answered the phone on its second ring.

"Guess what, honey?" My husband's voice quivered.

"What?" My heartbeat quickened and I started to perspire; I knew what "Guess what?" meant.

"We've been transferred," my husband said.

"No way," I said, "I'm not moving again."

I heard a sharp intake of breath on the line as my husband tried to gauge my degree of seriousness.

"But honey, you have to," he said. "I've REALLY been transferred; I leave in a week."

I dropped the phone.

***

In the evening we broke the news to Shane and Erin. Experience told us to approach the subject in a positive manner.

"Kids, remember when we told you we wouldn't always live here," we began.

That caught their attention.

"Well, Daddy's been transferred and..."

We didn't get any further. Both children burst into tears--so much for experience and a positive attitude.

After a ten minute family cry, everyone finally calmed down enough to talk.

The children were full of questions.

"Where will we live? Will we still go to school? Are there houses there? Kids?"

My little girl walked through the kitchen, touching things.

"Will we take the stove?" she said.

"Yes," I replied.

"Will we take the table and the microwave?"

"Yes."

"Will we take the cupboards?"

"No, we'll leave the cupboards."

A new flood of tears.

"But I LIKE these cupboards!"

I tried to comfort her. I explained that we would take all her toys and her clothes and our furniture, but we would leave the things that belong to the house, such as carpets, cupboards, and the drawers built into her bedroom wall.

It was a long evening.

***

Images tumbled one over another that night when I tried to sleep. Were we doing the right thing, uprooting the children again? This would be my son's fourth move and my daughter's third. Will my children have any roots?

I grew up in a small town, living in the same house until I moved away at the age of eighteen. I had one best friend all through elementary and high school.

We shared everything—secrets, books, and clothes, and we double-dated. My best friend even spent a good part of each summer with me at my parents' cottage. We played in the sun during the day and fought off June bugs together on our way to the outhouse at night.

My paternal grandparents lived in the century-old farmhouse with my family, and a string of aunts, uncles and cousins from nearby houses often dropped in to visit.

As a child, I knew I belonged within a tight framework of family and close friends. Life was constant.

Even now, if someone asks where I'm from, I offer the name of my home town and add, "It's a nice little town. Quiet."

What will my children say?

"Canada," or "I'm not really sure," or "I never lived in one place long enough to have a home town."

Will they feel cheated? Will they resent my husband and me because we moved them from town to town, from province to province? I hope not.

I hope the roots we do give Shane and Erin will more than compensate for the mobile lifestyle to which they must constantly adapt.

We give our children emotional roots by showing them what a husband and wife, mother and father, mean to each other. We offer them a stable love that many children do not have, standing together when we say "yes", and when we say "no".

We teach our children that HOME is more than a dwelling-place of cement, wood, and glass; it's the network of love, support, and understanding shared by the family inside the four walls. Family unity can remain strong even when the physical HOME changes shape.

I hope my children are learning this.

A few years ago my husband and I built a cottage at the same beach where my parents' former cottage still stands.

Shane and Erin swim in the cool salt water of Northumberland Strait, dive off Surprise Rock—so named when I was a little girl, and play with their cousins from neighboring cottages.

They pick sandfire greens in the marsh, eat blueberries and wild strawberries that grow in the fields, and fall asleep at night listening to the "grown-ups" talk in our cottage kitchen.

Summers at the beach offer my children a sense of security, of continuity.

They know that no matter how many houses they live in, or how many schools they have to be the "new kids" at, they'll always have their summers at our cottage, only fifty kilometers from relatives they rarely see the remainder of the year.

Maybe when Shane and Erin are grown and someone asks where they're from, they'll say, "Our family moved around a lot, but we had great summers."

Maybe they'll mention our cottage, the ocean, marshmallows roasted on a stick thrust into an open fire, and raindrops pattering on our cottage roof.

Those aren't bad roots.

But back to the present. The movers will soon arrive. They'll pack our belongings into crates and boxes, and then load them onto a huge van.

We'll wander through our house one last time, perhaps rescue a stray teddy-bear or find the gold earring I lost six months ago.

We'll shed more tears when we say good-bye to neighbors and dear friends, but we'll continue on the road to our new home.

In time, we'll adjust and feel comfortable with new buildings and new faces.

In time, Erin may learn to LIKE the cupboards in the new kitchen.

In time, we'll prepare to move again.

MOM, CAN WE HAVE A PUPPY?

Last winter, friends of mine bought their little boy a six-week-old puppy. It was cute—a roly-poly ball of fluff. My children loved it.

"Mom, could we have a puppy?" they said. "We'll do all the work. We'll walk it and feed it and clean up after it. We promise."

"I'll think about it," I said.

That night, after the children were in bed, my husband and I discussed their request.

"Maybe it is time to get a dog," I said. "It might be good for Shane and Erin."

My husband agreed. We both had fond memories of our own childhood pets; I always had a dog and a cat or two, and my husband had a dog plus a raccoon duo named Bonnie and Clyde.

Our conversation became peppered with bumper-sticker quotes.

"Every child needs a dog," I said.

"Having a pet is a good way to learn to be responsible," my husband added.

"A dog has so much affection to give; it loves you no matter what." We piped that one in unison, then grinned at each other like fools.

"Okay, children," I said the next morning. "We'll get a dog."

Shane and Erin cheered.

"But," I continued, "let's wait until spring."

Spring arrived and my husband's job transfer put a halt to our plan.

"We'll wait until we're settled in our new home," I said. "Then we'll find a dog."

At first, Shane and Erin didn't want a dog. They wanted a puppy. Any puppy.

They didn't care about puddles on the carpet and plaintive puppy-whines in the night. They wouldn't mind chewed sneakers, shredded furniture, and soggy rawhide bones on their beds.

However, I decided I was past the puppy stage in my life. We'd buy a dog—one already trained.

It's not that I don't lové puppies. I do. They're cute, playful and affectionate, but I'm familiar with the reality of raising one.

Before my husband and I had children (a whole NEW reality), we owned Tara—a beautiful little Beagle with long silky ears, sleek brown fur, and a definite mind of her own.

Tara took over our house and our lives.

She went everywhere with us. She slept on our laps, in the middle of our bed, and on my souvenir-of-Scotland velveteen pillow.

She howled at us if we reprimanded her, wouldn't come when she was called, and messed on our living room carpet. (She had chewed pink insulation when she was a pup and it left her with a delicate digestive system.)

She wasn't allowed dog food, only boiled rice with chicken or tuna mixed in—vet's orders. So Tara ate like the queen she thought she was, but she still had problems, thus the messes on our carpet.

We loved her anyway. She was like a wayward child. She tested our patience and our loyalty. (Good training for our Shane and Erin future.)

Unfortunately, by the time Shane was born, Tara's accidents had increased in frequency and we finally had to make the decision to give her away.

We found a good home for her, though, on a farm. She had lots of freedom there, and another dog for company. What better life?

We missed her a lot, but we had to think about the little blond boy who spent his days crawling around on our carpets, putting anything and everything into his mouth.

During the next few years we were busy with babies and toddlers and preschool imps. No time to think about a dog.

Now we're ready. Our children are old enough to assume some responsibility in caring for a pet, and my husband and I learned valuable lessons from our mistakes with Tara. We weren't as firm with her as we should have been.

Tara believed she was human and should be treated accordingly. Unfortunately, we believed it, too. We were young and didn't know any better.

We're older and wiser now. We know how to be both firm and loving. (We've had plenty of experience with our children.)

We won't repeat our mistakes this time.

This time the dog will be a dog—a great playmate for Shane and Erin, a loving companion for the entire family, a trusted and loyal friend—but a DOG, after all.

We'll set the ground rules early and stick to them. We'll all be happier.

***

We moved into our new home and started the search. At the local animal shelter we were offered a Great Dane or our choice of cute Labrador Retriever pups.

"No thanks; too big for us. We want something small".

"How about this two-year-old, long-haired Terrier?" I asked.

"No, she's afraid of children."

Shane and Erin were disappointed when we arrived home without a dog.

"We'll never get a pet," they said.

"Yes, we will, "I promised, "just as soon as we move to the cottage. It will be great there. Life is relaxed, the furniture is old, and we'll have time to spend with a new pet. That's important."

We settled into a summer routine and called another shelter. They had a few possibilities.

My husband and I decided to leave our children with my cousin at the cottage. We knew Shane and Erin weren't particular about dog size; they'd have lugged the Great Dane home and been content.

At this shelter we were introduced to Becky, a two-year-old, long-haired, medium-sized mama. We also met Patches, a Paul Bunyan version of Benji. Then we spied Chiquita, a year-old Terrier-Dachshund mix, who stood up on her hind legs for attention. Cute. Little. Fully-trained. That was our dog.

We signed the necessary papers and I carried Chiquita out to the car.

Shane and Erin bounced off the cottage walls when they saw the dog. A dog of their own! They could hardly believe their good fortune. We were the best parents in the world. They would love us forever, almost as much as they would love their dog!

We discussed names. Chiquita wasn't right. The lady at the shelter had named her that. What about Chi-Chi? No, too cutesy. The dog had four white paws. What about Boots? No. Whisper? No. Finally I suggested Tara.

"Tara." The children tried the sound of it a few times and liked it, so we have another Tara.

We hope she'll settle in. She's still shy. She trembles if there are too many people around her. She doesn't run away. She hasn't touched our slippers or the children's toys, and she knows what the great outdoors is for.

We've definitely started off on the right foot (or paw, as it is).

We're all content. Shane and Erin have a pet, the shelter dog has a home, and my husband and I are still in control of our lives. What more could I ask for?

Well, I could ask for a cup of coffee. I'd get it myself, but I can't stand up. Tara is asleep on my lap and she doesn't like to be disturbed.

Sh-h-h-h…..

###

ABOUT THE AUTHOR

Sylvia Morice writes fiction, creative non-fiction and poetry. Her work has been published in Canadian magazines, periodicals and newspapers and as a Chapbook *Wages of Sin* by Wild East Publishing.

She has recently published several eBooks, available from most online book retailers. Postcards From Home is Sylvia's first paperback book.

After many years of moving around from town to town, Sylvia is now living back in her hometown of Sackville NB, where she continues to write.

Connect with Sylvia Online:
Website: sylviamorice.com
Email: sylvia@sylviamorice.com
Twitter: twitter.com/sylviamorice
Blog: sylviamorice.wordpress.com

Made in the USA
Charleston, SC
05 December 2012